MW00898633

UNLOCK YOUR DREAMS

GUIDED DREAM JOURNAL FOR BLACK WOMEN WITH PROMPTS TO INTERPRET AND REFLECT ON YOUR DREAMS

Copyright © 2021 Stress Less Press. All rights
reserved. No part of this book may be reproduced or transmitted in any
form by any means, electronic or mechanical, including
photocopying, scanning and recording,
or by any information storage and retrieval system,
without permission in writing from the publisher,
except for the review for inclusion in a magazine, newspaper or broadcast.

CHECK OUT OUR OTHER SELF CARE BOOKS

SELF CARE WORKBOOK FOR BLACK WOMEN
A 150+ page activity book covering mental, physical, spiritual and emotional self help practices. Complete with a 12-month planner and guided journal

EMOTIONAL SELF CARE FOR BLACK WOMEN
A self help activity book to address the thoughts, beliefs and triggers which affect your emotions and behavior

SPIRITUAL SELF CARE FOR BLACK WOMEN
A guided journal and 12-month planner with in-depth self reflection and spirituality activities

SELF CARE PLANNER & JOURNAL FOR BLACK WOMEN
A simple self care organizer and reflective journal

Stress Less Press are a Black-owned independent publisher. If you enjoy this book, please consider supporting us by leaving a review on Amazon!

INTRODUCTION
LET'S TALK ABOUT DREAMS

We've all been there: you wake up in a panic after dreaming you're being chased by a monster. You frantically search Google trying to understand what it means. Some sources will tell you that being chased in your dreams means you're running from debt or addiction, others say the 'monster' is a manifestation of an emotion you're suppressing. But the most important interpretation is what the dream means to **you**.

Our fascination with dreams is nothing new, though. It's happened for centuries; our ancestors in ancient Egypt believed dreams were a medium between humans and the Gods. The Greeks and Romans were convinced that dreams could predict the future.

No matter what you choose to believe, recording and analyzing your dreams can offer great insight into your inner self. It can allow you to spot patterns and recurring themes which are usually relevant in your 'conscious' life. Scientists have found that when we dream, we continue to experience thoughts and feelings, but more intensely: our mistakes, our achievements, our hopes. Dreams also allow us to tap into our subconscious as our prefrontal cortex - which controls rational thought - is dormant. So when we study our dreams, it can help us with personal growth, problem solving and even processing trauma.

It's estimated that we have roughly 3-6 dreams in one night and around 95% of these dreams are forgotten the following morning. However, our ability to recall dreams can be increased through journaling - it's is a real skill that requires practice over time.

So put this journal on your nightstand and using the prompts provided, routinely scribble/draw your thoughts and memories as soon as you wake up. You'll be surprised what you learn about yourself, Sis.

COMMON DREAM INTERPRETATIONS

It goes without saying that dreams are best interpreted by the individual. However there are some common scenarios and symbols that many people dream about - and it's worth knowing what these might mean.

Falling in a dream can be interpreted that you're unhappy with how a certain event has played out in your conscious life or that you feel overwhelmed and need to slow down.

Being naked can point to a feeling of imposter syndrome, meaning you fear being 'exposed' for being incompetent in some way.

Being chased can represent your desire to run away from your problems (relationships, friendships or situationships) rather than face them head-on. It could also reflect a past trauma coming back to rear it's nasty head.

Losing teeth is usually linked to some kind of anxiety, that could be about your appearance, speaking your truth or feeling humiliated about something you've said or done.

Taking a test (or running late for one, or being unprepared for one) might show up in your dreams if you feel underprepared for life in general or are not ready to move on to the next chapter.

Infidelity in dreams... Now hold up, Sis. This does <u>not</u> mean you're being cheated on. It more likely means you feel a lack of trust or loyalty with your partner. Alternatively, you might just need to work on communication in your relationship.

Death is, of course, a very distressing thing to dream about but try not to worry about it too much! It's more symbolic of a situation or habit that needs to metaphorically 'die'.

Dreams are illustrations from the book your soul is writing about you

MARSHA NORMAN

DATE:

THE TYPE OF DREAM

○ Nightmare   ○ Fantasy   ○ Symbolic   ○ Lucid

ANY SLEEP AIDS USED?

○ No   ○ Yes: _____

SLEEP DURATION

_____ hours

WHAT HAPPENED IN THE DREAM?

_____
_____
_____
_____
_____
_____
_____

WHAT'S YOUR INTERPRETATION?

_____
_____
_____
_____
_____
_____

REFLECTIVE DRAWING

A quick sketch that represents what happened or how you're feeling

WHAT FEELINGS IT BROUGHT UP

○ Anger   ○ Anxiety   ○ Peace

○ Fear   ○ Happiness   ○ Love

○ Shame   ○ Freedom   ○ Confusion

○ Sadness   ○ Arousal   ○ Other: _____

WHAT RECURRING THEMES OR SYMBOLS HAVE YOU IDENTIFIED?

DATE:

THE TYPE OF DREAM

○ Nightmare ○ Fantasy ○ Symbolic ○ Lucid

ANY SLEEP AIDS USED?

○ No ○ Yes: _____

SLEEP DURATION

_____ hours

WHAT HAPPENED IN THE DREAM?

_____
_____
_____
_____
_____
_____
_____

WHAT'S YOUR INTERPRETATION?

_____
_____
_____
_____
_____
_____
_____

REFLECTIVE DRAWING

A quick sketch that represents what happened or how you're feeling

WHAT FEELINGS IT BROUGHT UP

○ Anger   ○ Anxiety   ○ Peace

○ Fear   ○ Happiness   ○ Love

○ Shame   ○ Freedom   ○ Confusion

○ Sadness   ○ Arousal   ○ Other: _____

WHAT RECURRING THEMES OR SYMBOLS HAVE YOU IDENTIFIED?

_____

_____

_____

_____

_____

DATE:

THE TYPE OF DREAM

○ Nightmare ○ Fantasy ○ Symbolic ○ Lucid

ANY SLEEP AIDS USED?

○ No ○ Yes: _____

SLEEP DURATION

_____ hours

WHAT HAPPENED IN THE DREAM?

_____
_____
_____
_____
_____
_____

WHAT'S YOUR INTERPRETATION?

_____
_____
_____
_____
_____
_____

REFLECTIVE DRAWING

A quick sketch that represents what happened or how you're feeling

WHAT FEELINGS IT BROUGHT UP

- ◯ Anger
- ◯ Fear
- ◯ Shame
- ◯ Sadness

- ◯ Anxiety
- ◯ Happiness
- ◯ Freedom
- ◯ Arousal

- ◯ Peace
- ◯ Love
- ◯ Confusion
- ◯ Other: _____

WHAT RECURRING THEMES OR SYMBOLS HAVE YOU IDENTIFIED?

_____

_____

_____

_____

DATE:

THE TYPE OF DREAM

○ Nightmare ○ Fantasy ○ Symbolic ○ Lucid

ANY SLEEP AIDS USED?

○ No ○ Yes: _____

SLEEP DURATION

_____ hours

WHAT HAPPENED IN THE DREAM?

_____
_____
_____
_____
_____
_____
_____

WHAT'S YOUR INTERPRETATION?

_____
_____
_____
_____
_____
_____

REFLECTIVE DRAWING

A quick sketch that represents what happened or how you're feeling

WHAT FEELINGS IT BROUGHT UP

- ○ Anger
- ○ Fear
- ○ Shame
- ○ Sadness

- ○ Anxiety
- ○ Happiness
- ○ Freedom
- ○ Arousal

- ○ Peace
- ○ Love
- ○ Confusion
- ○ Other: _____

WHAT RECURRING THEMES OR SYMBOLS HAVE YOU IDENTIFIED?

DATE:

THE TYPE OF DREAM

○ Nightmare ○ Fantasy ○ Symbolic ○ Lucid

ANY SLEEP AIDS USED?

○ No ○ Yes: _____

SLEEP DURATION

_____ hours

WHAT HAPPENED IN THE DREAM?

_____
_____
_____
_____
_____
_____
_____

WHAT'S YOUR INTERPRETATION?

_____
_____
_____
_____
_____
_____
_____

REFLECTIVE DRAWING

A quick sketch that represents what happened or how you're feeling

WHAT FEELINGS IT BROUGHT UP

- ○ Anger
- ○ Fear
- ○ Shame
- ○ Sadness

- ○ Anxiety
- ○ Happiness
- ○ Freedom
- ○ Arousal

- ○ Peace
- ○ Love
- ○ Confusion
- ○ Other: _____

WHAT RECURRING THEMES OR SYMBOLS HAVE YOU IDENTIFIED?

_____

_____

_____

_____

_____

DATE:

THE TYPE OF DREAM

○ Nightmare ○ Fantasy ○ Symbolic ○ Lucid

ANY SLEEP AIDS USED?

○ No ○ Yes: _____

SLEEP DURATION

_____ hours

WHAT HAPPENED IN THE DREAM?

_____
_____
_____
_____
_____
_____
_____

WHAT'S YOUR INTERPRETATION?

_____
_____
_____
_____
_____
_____
_____

REFLECTIVE DRAWING

A quick sketch that represents what happened or how you're feeling

WHAT FEELINGS IT BROUGHT UP

- ○ Anger
- ○ Fear
- ○ Shame
- ○ Sadness

- ○ Anxiety
- ○ Happiness
- ○ Freedom
- ○ Arousal

- ○ Peace
- ○ Love
- ○ Confusion
- ○ Other: _____

WHAT RECURRING THEMES OR SYMBOLS HAVE YOU IDENTIFIED?

DATE:

THE TYPE OF DREAM

◯ Nightmare   ◯ Fantasy   ◯ Symbolic   ◯ Lucid

ANY SLEEP AIDS USED?

◯ No   ◯ Yes: _____

SLEEP DURATION

_____ hours

WHAT HAPPENED IN THE DREAM?

_____
_____
_____
_____
_____
_____

WHAT'S YOUR INTERPRETATION?

_____
_____
_____
_____
_____
_____

REFLECTIVE DRAWING

A quick sketch that represents what happened or how you're feeling

WHAT FEELINGS IT BROUGHT UP

○ Anger   ○ Anxiety   ○ Peace

○ Fear   ○ Happiness   ○ Love

○ Shame   ○ Freedom   ○ Confusion

○ Sadness   ○ Arousal   ○ Other: _____

WHAT RECURRING THEMES OR SYMBOLS HAVE YOU IDENTIFIED?

_____

_____

_____

_____

DATE:

THE TYPE OF DREAM

○ Nightmare   ○ Fantasy   ○ Symbolic   ○ Lucid

ANY SLEEP AIDS USED?

○ No   ○ Yes: _____

SLEEP DURATION

_____ hours

WHAT HAPPENED IN THE DREAM?

_____
_____
_____
_____
_____
_____
_____

WHAT'S YOUR INTERPRETATION?

_____
_____
_____
_____
_____
_____
_____

REFLECTIVE DRAWING

A quick sketch that represents what happened or how you're feeling

WHAT FEELINGS IT BROUGHT UP

- ○ Anger
- ○ Fear
- ○ Shame
- ○ Sadness

- ○ Anxiety
- ○ Happiness
- ○ Freedom
- ○ Arousal

- ○ Peace
- ○ Love
- ○ Confusion
- ○ Other: _____

WHAT RECURRING THEMES OR SYMBOLS HAVE YOU IDENTIFIED?

DATE:

THE TYPE OF DREAM

○ Nightmare ○ Fantasy ○ Symbolic ○ Lucid

ANY SLEEP AIDS USED?

○ No ○ Yes: _____

SLEEP DURATION

_____ hours

WHAT HAPPENED IN THE DREAM?

_____
_____
_____
_____
_____
_____

WHAT'S YOUR INTERPRETATION?

_____
_____
_____
_____
_____
_____

REFLECTIVE DRAWING

A quick sketch that represents what happened or how you're feeling

WHAT FEELINGS IT BROUGHT UP

○ Anger   ○ Anxiety   ○ Peace

○ Fear   ○ Happiness   ○ Love

○ Shame   ○ Freedom   ○ Confusion

○ Sadness   ○ Arousal   ○ Other: _____

WHAT RECURRING THEMES OR SYMBOLS HAVE YOU IDENTIFIED?

_____

_____

_____

_____

DATE:

THE TYPE OF DREAM

○ Nightmare ○ Fantasy ○ Symbolic ○ Lucid

ANY SLEEP AIDS USED?

○ No ○ Yes: _____

SLEEP DURATION

_____ hours

WHAT HAPPENED IN THE DREAM?

_____
_____
_____
_____
_____
_____
_____

WHAT'S YOUR INTERPRETATION?

_____
_____
_____
_____
_____
_____
_____

REFLECTIVE DRAWING

A quick sketch that represents what happened or how you're feeling

WHAT FEELINGS IT BROUGHT UP

- ○ Anger
- ○ Fear
- ○ Shame
- ○ Sadness

- ○ Anxiety
- ○ Happiness
- ○ Freedom
- ○ Arousal

- ○ Peace
- ○ Love
- ○ Confusion
- ○ Other: _____

WHAT RECURRING THEMES OR SYMBOLS HAVE YOU IDENTIFIED?

DATE:

THE TYPE OF DREAM

○ Nightmare　○ Fantasy　○ Symbolic　○ Lucid

ANY SLEEP AIDS USED?

○ No　○ Yes: _____

SLEEP DURATION

_____ hours

WHAT HAPPENED IN THE DREAM?

_____
_____
_____
_____
_____
_____

WHAT'S YOUR INTERPRETATION?

_____
_____
_____
_____
_____

REFLECTIVE DRAWING

A quick sketch that represents what happened or how you're feeling

WHAT FEELINGS IT BROUGHT UP

- ○ Anger
- ○ Fear
- ○ Shame
- ○ Sadness

- ○ Anxiety
- ○ Happiness
- ○ Freedom
- ○ Arousal

- ○ Peace
- ○ Love
- ○ Confusion
- ○ Other: _____

WHAT RECURRING THEMES OR SYMBOLS HAVE YOU IDENTIFIED?

DATE:

THE TYPE OF DREAM

○ Nightmare   ○ Fantasy   ○ Symbolic   ○ Lucid

ANY SLEEP AIDS USED?

○ No   ○ Yes: _____

SLEEP DURATION

_____ hours

WHAT HAPPENED IN THE DREAM?

_____
_____
_____
_____
_____
_____

WHAT'S YOUR INTERPRETATION?

_____
_____
_____
_____
_____
_____

REFLECTIVE DRAWING

A quick sketch that represents what happened or how you're feeling

WHAT FEELINGS IT BROUGHT UP

- ○ Anger
- ○ Fear
- ○ Shame
- ○ Sadness

- ○ Anxiety
- ○ Happiness
- ○ Freedom
- ○ Arousal

- ○ Peace
- ○ Love
- ○ Confusion
- ○ Other: _____

WHAT RECURRING THEMES OR SYMBOLS HAVE YOU IDENTIFIED?

_____

_____

_____

_____

DATE:

THE TYPE OF DREAM

○ Nightmare   ○ Fantasy   ○ Symbolic   ○ Lucid

ANY SLEEP AIDS USED?

○ No   ○ Yes: _____

SLEEP DURATION

_____ hours

WHAT HAPPENED IN THE DREAM?

_____
_____
_____
_____
_____
_____
_____

WHAT'S YOUR INTERPRETATION?

_____
_____
_____
_____
_____
_____

REFLECTIVE DRAWING

A quick sketch that represents what happened or how you're feeling

WHAT FEELINGS IT BROUGHT UP

- ○ Anger
- ○ Fear
- ○ Shame
- ○ Sadness

- ○ Anxiety
- ○ Happiness
- ○ Freedom
- ○ Arousal

- ○ Peace
- ○ Love
- ○ Confusion
- ○ Other: _____

WHAT RECURRING THEMES OR SYMBOLS HAVE YOU IDENTIFIED?

_____

_____

_____

_____

DATE:

THE TYPE OF DREAM

○ Nightmare ○ Fantasy ○ Symbolic ○ Lucid

ANY SLEEP AIDS USED?

○ No ○ Yes: _____

SLEEP DURATION

_____ hours

WHAT HAPPENED IN THE DREAM?

_____
_____
_____
_____
_____
_____

WHAT'S YOUR INTERPRETATION?

_____
_____
_____
_____
_____
_____

REFLECTIVE DRAWING

A quick sketch that represents what happened or how you're feeling

WHAT FEELINGS IT BROUGHT UP

○ Anger   ○ Anxiety   ○ Peace

○ Fear   ○ Happiness   ○ Love

○ Shame   ○ Freedom   ○ Confusion

○ Sadness   ○ Arousal   ○ Other: _____

WHAT RECURRING THEMES OR SYMBOLS HAVE YOU IDENTIFIED?

_____

_____

_____

_____

DATE:

THE TYPE OF DREAM

○ Nightmare   ○ Fantasy   ○ Symbolic   ○ Lucid

ANY SLEEP AIDS USED?

○ No   ○ Yes: _____

SLEEP DURATION

_____ hours

WHAT HAPPENED IN THE DREAM?

_____
_____
_____
_____
_____
_____

WHAT'S YOUR INTERPRETATION?

_____
_____
_____
_____
_____
_____

REFLECTIVE DRAWING

A quick sketch that represents what happened or how you're feeling

WHAT FEELINGS IT BROUGHT UP

- ○ Anger
- ○ Fear
- ○ Shame
- ○ Sadness

- ○ Anxiety
- ○ Happiness
- ○ Freedom
- ○ Arousal

- ○ Peace
- ○ Love
- ○ Confusion
- ○ Other: _____

WHAT RECURRING THEMES OR SYMBOLS HAVE YOU IDENTIFIED?

_____

_____

_____

_____

DATE:

THE TYPE OF DREAM

○ Nightmare   ○ Fantasy   ○ Symbolic   ○ Lucid

ANY SLEEP AIDS USED?

○ No   ○ Yes: _____

SLEEP DURATION

_____ hours

WHAT HAPPENED IN THE DREAM?

_____
_____
_____
_____
_____
_____

WHAT'S YOUR INTERPRETATION?

_____
_____
_____
_____
_____
_____

REFLECTIVE DRAWING

A quick sketch that represents what happened or how you're feeling

WHAT FEELINGS IT BROUGHT UP

○ Anger   ○ Anxiety   ○ Peace

○ Fear   ○ Happiness   ○ Love

○ Shame   ○ Freedom   ○ Confusion

○ Sadness   ○ Arousal   ○ Other: _____

WHAT RECURRING THEMES OR SYMBOLS HAVE YOU IDENTIFIED?

_____

_____

_____

_____

DATE:

THE TYPE OF DREAM

○ Nightmare ○ Fantasy ○ Symbolic ○ Lucid

ANY SLEEP AIDS USED?

○ No ○ Yes: _____

SLEEP DURATION

_____ hours

WHAT HAPPENED IN THE DREAM?

_____
_____
_____
_____
_____
_____

WHAT'S YOUR INTERPRETATION?

_____
_____
_____
_____
_____
_____

REFLECTIVE DRAWING

A quick sketch that represents what happened or how you're feeling

WHAT FEELINGS IT BROUGHT UP

- ○ Anger
- ○ Fear
- ○ Shame
- ○ Sadness

- ○ Anxiety
- ○ Happiness
- ○ Freedom
- ○ Arousal

- ○ Peace
- ○ Love
- ○ Confusion
- ○ Other: _____

WHAT RECURRING THEMES OR SYMBOLS HAVE YOU IDENTIFIED?

DATE:

THE TYPE OF DREAM

○ Nightmare ○ Fantasy ○ Symbolic ○ Lucid

ANY SLEEP AIDS USED?

○ No ○ Yes: _____

SLEEP DURATION

_____ hours

WHAT HAPPENED IN THE DREAM?

_____
_____
_____
_____
_____
_____
_____

WHAT'S YOUR INTERPRETATION?

_____
_____
_____
_____
_____
_____
_____

REFLECTIVE DRAWING

A quick sketch that represents what happened or how you're feeling

WHAT FEELINGS IT BROUGHT UP

- ○ Anger
- ○ Fear
- ○ Shame
- ○ Sadness

- ○ Anxiety
- ○ Happiness
- ○ Freedom
- ○ Arousal

- ○ Peace
- ○ Love
- ○ Confusion
- ○ Other: _____

WHAT RECURRING THEMES OR SYMBOLS HAVE YOU IDENTIFIED?

DATE:

THE TYPE OF DREAM

○ Nightmare   ○ Fantasy   ○ Symbolic   ○ Lucid

ANY SLEEP AIDS USED?

○ No   ○ Yes: _____

SLEEP DURATION

_____ hours

WHAT HAPPENED IN THE DREAM?

_____
_____
_____
_____
_____
_____
_____

WHAT'S YOUR INTERPRETATION?

_____
_____
_____
_____
_____
_____
_____

REFLECTIVE DRAWING

A quick sketch that represents what happened or how you're feeling

WHAT FEELINGS IT BROUGHT UP

- ○ Anger
- ○ Fear
- ○ Shame
- ○ Sadness

- ○ Anxiety
- ○ Happiness
- ○ Freedom
- ○ Arousal

- ○ Peace
- ○ Love
- ○ Confusion
- ○ Other: _____

WHAT RECURRING THEMES OR SYMBOLS HAVE YOU IDENTIFIED?

THE TYPE OF DREAM

○ Nightmare   ○ Fantasy   ○ Symbolic   ○ Lucid

ANY SLEEP AIDS USED?

○ No   ○ Yes: _____

SLEEP DURATION

_____ hours

WHAT HAPPENED IN THE DREAM?

_____
_____
_____
_____
_____
_____

WHAT'S YOUR INTERPRETATION?

_____
_____
_____
_____
_____
_____

REFLECTIVE DRAWING

A quick sketch that represents what happened or how you're feeling

WHAT FEELINGS IT BROUGHT UP

- ○ Anger
- ○ Fear
- ○ Shame
- ○ Sadness

- ○ Anxiety
- ○ Happiness
- ○ Freedom
- ○ Arousal

- ○ Peace
- ○ Love
- ○ Confusion
- ○ Other: _____

WHAT RECURRING THEMES OR SYMBOLS HAVE YOU IDENTIFIED?

_____

_____

_____

_____

DATE:

THE TYPE OF DREAM

○ Nightmare ○ Fantasy ○ Symbolic ○ Lucid

ANY SLEEP AIDS USED?

○ No ○ Yes: _____

SLEEP DURATION

_____ hours

WHAT HAPPENED IN THE DREAM?

_____
_____
_____
_____
_____
_____

WHAT'S YOUR INTERPRETATION?

_____
_____
_____
_____
_____
_____

REFLECTIVE DRAWING

A quick sketch that represents what happened or how you're feeling

WHAT FEELINGS IT BROUGHT UP

○ Anger   ○ Anxiety   ○ Peace

○ Fear   ○ Happiness   ○ Love

○ Shame   ○ Freedom   ○ Confusion

○ Sadness   ○ Arousal   ○ Other: _____

WHAT RECURRING THEMES OR SYMBOLS HAVE YOU IDENTIFIED?

_____

_____

_____

_____

DATE:

THE TYPE OF DREAM

○ Nightmare ○ Fantasy ○ Symbolic ○ Lucid

ANY SLEEP AIDS USED?

○ No ○ Yes: _____

SLEEP DURATION

_____ hours

WHAT HAPPENED IN THE DREAM?

_____
_____
_____
_____
_____
_____

WHAT'S YOUR INTERPRETATION?

_____
_____
_____
_____
_____

REFLECTIVE DRAWING

A quick sketch that represents what happened or how you're feeling

WHAT FEELINGS IT BROUGHT UP

- ○ Anger
- ○ Fear
- ○ Shame
- ○ Sadness

- ○ Anxiety
- ○ Happiness
- ○ Freedom
- ○ Arousal

- ○ Peace
- ○ Love
- ○ Confusion
- ○ Other: _____

WHAT RECURRING THEMES OR SYMBOLS HAVE YOU IDENTIFIED?

_____

_____

_____

_____

DATE:

THE TYPE OF DREAM

○ Nightmare ○ Fantasy ○ Symbolic ○ Lucid

ANY SLEEP AIDS USED?

○ No   ○ Yes: _____

SLEEP DURATION

_____ hours

WHAT HAPPENED IN THE DREAM?

_____
_____
_____
_____
_____
_____

WHAT'S YOUR INTERPRETATION?

_____
_____
_____
_____
_____
_____

REFLECTIVE DRAWING

A quick sketch that represents what happened or how you're feeling

WHAT FEELINGS IT BROUGHT UP

○ Anger   ○ Anxiety   ○ Peace

○ Fear   ○ Happiness   ○ Love

○ Shame   ○ Freedom   ○ Confusion

○ Sadness   ○ Arousal   ○ Other: _____

WHAT RECURRING THEMES OR SYMBOLS HAVE YOU IDENTIFIED?

_____

_____

_____

_____

_____

DATE:

THE TYPE OF DREAM

○ Nightmare ○ Fantasy ○ Symbolic ○ Lucid

ANY SLEEP AIDS USED?

○ No ○ Yes: _____

SLEEP DURATION

_____ hours

WHAT HAPPENED IN THE DREAM?

_____
_____
_____
_____
_____
_____

WHAT'S YOUR INTERPRETATION?

_____
_____
_____
_____
_____
_____

REFLECTIVE DRAWING

A quick sketch that represents what happened or how you're feeling

WHAT FEELINGS IT BROUGHT UP

○ Anger   ○ Anxiety   ○ Peace

○ Fear   ○ Happiness   ○ Love

○ Shame   ○ Freedom   ○ Confusion

○ Sadness   ○ Arousal   ○ Other: _____

WHAT RECURRING THEMES OR SYMBOLS HAVE YOU IDENTIFIED?

_____

_____

_____

_____

DATE:

THE TYPE OF DREAM

○ Nightmare   ○ Fantasy   ○ Symbolic   ○ Lucid

ANY SLEEP AIDS USED?

○ No   ○ Yes: _____

SLEEP DURATION

_____ hours

WHAT HAPPENED IN THE DREAM?

_____
_____
_____
_____
_____
_____

WHAT'S YOUR INTERPRETATION?

_____
_____
_____
_____
_____
_____

REFLECTIVE DRAWING

A quick sketch that represents what happened or how you're feeling

WHAT FEELINGS IT BROUGHT UP

○ Anger   ○ Anxiety   ○ Peace

○ Fear   ○ Happiness   ○ Love

○ Shame   ○ Freedom   ○ Confusion

○ Sadness   ○ Arousal   ○ Other: _____

WHAT RECURRING THEMES OR SYMBOLS HAVE YOU IDENTIFIED?

_____

_____

_____

_____

_____

DATE:

THE TYPE OF DREAM

○ Nightmare   ○ Fantasy   ○ Symbolic   ○ Lucid

ANY SLEEP AIDS USED?

○ No   ○ Yes: _____

SLEEP DURATION

_____ hours

WHAT HAPPENED IN THE DREAM?

_____

_____

_____

_____

_____

_____

_____

WHAT'S YOUR INTERPRETATION?

_____

_____

_____

_____

_____

_____

REFLECTIVE DRAWING

A quick sketch that represents what happened or how you're feeling

WHAT FEELINGS IT BROUGHT UP

- ○ Anger
- ○ Fear
- ○ Shame
- ○ Sadness

- ○ Anxiety
- ○ Happiness
- ○ Freedom
- ○ Arousal

- ○ Peace
- ○ Love
- ○ Confusion
- ○ Other: _____

WHAT RECURRING THEMES OR SYMBOLS HAVE YOU IDENTIFIED?

_____

_____

_____

_____

DATE:

THE TYPE OF DREAM

○ Nightmare ○ Fantasy ○ Symbolic ○ Lucid

ANY SLEEP AIDS USED?

○ No ○ Yes: _____

SLEEP DURATION

_____ hours

WHAT HAPPENED IN THE DREAM?

_____
_____
_____
_____
_____
_____

WHAT'S YOUR INTERPRETATION?

_____
_____
_____
_____
_____
_____

REFLECTIVE DRAWING

A quick sketch that represents what happened or how you're feeling

WHAT FEELINGS IT BROUGHT UP

- ○ Anger
- ○ Fear
- ○ Shame
- ○ Sadness

- ○ Anxiety
- ○ Happiness
- ○ Freedom
- ○ Arousal

- ○ Peace
- ○ Love
- ○ Confusion
- ○ Other: _____

WHAT RECURRING THEMES OR SYMBOLS HAVE YOU IDENTIFIED?

DATE:

THE TYPE OF DREAM

○ Nightmare ○ Fantasy ○ Symbolic ○ Lucid

ANY SLEEP AIDS USED?

○ No ○ Yes: _____

SLEEP DURATION

_____ hours

WHAT HAPPENED IN THE DREAM?

_____
_____
_____
_____
_____
_____
_____

WHAT'S YOUR INTERPRETATION?

_____
_____
_____
_____
_____
_____
_____

REFLECTIVE DRAWING

A quick sketch that represents what happened or how you're feeling

WHAT FEELINGS IT BROUGHT UP

○ Anger   ○ Anxiety   ○ Peace

○ Fear   ○ Happiness   ○ Love

○ Shame   ○ Freedom   ○ Confusion

○ Sadness   ○ Arousal   ○ Other: _____

WHAT RECURRING THEMES OR SYMBOLS HAVE YOU IDENTIFIED?

_____

_____

_____

_____

DATE:

THE TYPE OF DREAM

○ Nightmare ○ Fantasy ○ Symbolic ○ Lucid

ANY SLEEP AIDS USED?

○ No ○ Yes: _____

SLEEP DURATION

_____ hours

WHAT HAPPENED IN THE DREAM?

_____
_____
_____
_____
_____
_____
_____

WHAT'S YOUR INTERPRETATION?

_____
_____
_____
_____
_____
_____

REFLECTIVE DRAWING

A quick sketch that represents what happened or how you're feeling

WHAT FEELINGS IT BROUGHT UP

○ Anger   ○ Anxiety   ○ Peace

○ Fear   ○ Happiness   ○ Love

○ Shame   ○ Freedom   ○ Confusion

○ Sadness   ○ Arousal   ○ Other: _____

WHAT RECURRING THEMES OR SYMBOLS HAVE YOU IDENTIFIED?

_____

_____

_____

_____

DATE:

THE TYPE OF DREAM

○ Nightmare   ○ Fantasy   ○ Symbolic   ○ Lucid

ANY SLEEP AIDS USED?

○ No   ○ Yes: _____

SLEEP DURATION

_____ hours

WHAT HAPPENED IN THE DREAM?

_____
_____
_____
_____
_____
_____

WHAT'S YOUR INTERPRETATION?

_____
_____
_____
_____
_____
_____

REFLECTIVE DRAWING

A quick sketch that represents what happened or how you're feeling

WHAT FEELINGS IT BROUGHT UP

- ○ Anger
- ○ Fear
- ○ Shame
- ○ Sadness

- ○ Anxiety
- ○ Happiness
- ○ Freedom
- ○ Arousal

- ○ Peace
- ○ Love
- ○ Confusion
- ○ Other: _____

WHAT RECURRING THEMES OR SYMBOLS HAVE YOU IDENTIFIED?

_____

_____

_____

_____

DATE:

THE TYPE OF DREAM

○ Nightmare ○ Fantasy ○ Symbolic ○ Lucid

ANY SLEEP AIDS USED?

○ No ○ Yes: _____

SLEEP DURATION

_____ hours

WHAT HAPPENED IN THE DREAM?

_____
_____
_____
_____
_____
_____

WHAT'S YOUR INTERPRETATION?

_____
_____
_____
_____
_____
_____

REFLECTIVE DRAWING

A quick sketch that represents what happened or how you're feeling

WHAT FEELINGS IT BROUGHT UP

- ○ Anger
- ○ Fear
- ○ Shame
- ○ Sadness

- ○ Anxiety
- ○ Happiness
- ○ Freedom
- ○ Arousal

- ○ Peace
- ○ Love
- ○ Confusion
- ○ Other: _____

WHAT RECURRING THEMES OR SYMBOLS HAVE YOU IDENTIFIED?

_____

_____

_____

_____

DATE:

THE TYPE OF DREAM

○ Nightmare ○ Fantasy ○ Symbolic ○ Lucid

ANY SLEEP AIDS USED?

○ No ○ Yes: _____

SLEEP DURATION

_____ hours

WHAT HAPPENED IN THE DREAM?

_____
_____
_____
_____
_____
_____

WHAT'S YOUR INTERPRETATION?

_____
_____
_____
_____
_____
_____

REFLECTIVE DRAWING

A quick sketch that represents what happened or how you're feeling

WHAT FEELINGS IT BROUGHT UP

○ Anger   ○ Anxiety   ○ Peace

○ Fear   ○ Happiness   ○ Love

○ Shame   ○ Freedom   ○ Confusion

○ Sadness   ○ Arousal   ○ Other: _____

WHAT RECURRING THEMES OR SYMBOLS HAVE YOU IDENTIFIED?

_____

_____

_____

_____

_____

DATE:

THE TYPE OF DREAM

○ Nightmare   ○ Fantasy   ○ Symbolic   ○ Lucid

ANY SLEEP AIDS USED?

○ No   ○ Yes: _____

SLEEP DURATION

_____ hours

WHAT HAPPENED IN THE DREAM?

_____
_____
_____
_____
_____
_____

WHAT'S YOUR INTERPRETATION?

_____
_____
_____
_____
_____

REFLECTIVE DRAWING

A quick sketch that represents what happened or how you're feeling

WHAT FEELINGS IT BROUGHT UP

○ Anger   ○ Anxiety   ○ Peace

○ Fear   ○ Happiness   ○ Love

○ Shame   ○ Freedom   ○ Confusion

○ Sadness   ○ Arousal   ○ Other: _____

WHAT RECURRING THEMES OR SYMBOLS HAVE YOU IDENTIFIED?

_____

_____

_____

_____

DATE:

THE TYPE OF DREAM

○ Nightmare ○ Fantasy ○ Symbolic ○ Lucid

ANY SLEEP AIDS USED?

○ No ○ Yes: _____

SLEEP DURATION

_____ hours

WHAT HAPPENED IN THE DREAM?

_____
_____
_____
_____
_____
_____

WHAT'S YOUR INTERPRETATION?

_____
_____
_____
_____
_____
_____
_____

REFLECTIVE DRAWING

A quick sketch that represents what happened or how you're feeling

WHAT FEELINGS IT BROUGHT UP

○ Anger   ○ Anxiety   ○ Peace

○ Fear   ○ Happiness   ○ Love

○ Shame   ○ Freedom   ○ Confusion

○ Sadness   ○ Arousal   ○ Other: _____

WHAT RECURRING THEMES OR SYMBOLS HAVE YOU IDENTIFIED?

_____

_____

_____

_____

DATE:

THE TYPE OF DREAM

○ Nightmare ○ Fantasy ○ Symbolic ○ Lucid

ANY SLEEP AIDS USED?

○ No ○ Yes: _____

SLEEP DURATION

_____ hours

WHAT HAPPENED IN THE DREAM?

_____
_____
_____
_____
_____
_____

WHAT'S YOUR INTERPRETATION?

_____
_____
_____
_____
_____
_____

REFLECTIVE DRAWING

A quick sketch that represents what happened or how you're feeling

WHAT FEELINGS IT BROUGHT UP

- ◯ Anger
- ◯ Fear
- ◯ Shame
- ◯ Sadness

- ◯ Anxiety
- ◯ Happiness
- ◯ Freedom
- ◯ Arousal

- ◯ Peace
- ◯ Love
- ◯ Confusion
- ◯ Other: _____

WHAT RECURRING THEMES OR SYMBOLS HAVE YOU IDENTIFIED?

_____

_____

_____

_____

_____

DATE:

THE TYPE OF DREAM

○ Nightmare ○ Fantasy ○ Symbolic ○ Lucid

ANY SLEEP AIDS USED?

○ No ○ Yes: _____

SLEEP DURATION

_____ hours

WHAT HAPPENED IN THE DREAM?

_____
_____
_____
_____
_____
_____
_____

WHAT'S YOUR INTERPRETATION?

_____
_____
_____
_____
_____
_____

REFLECTIVE DRAWING

A quick sketch that represents what happened or how you're feeling

WHAT FEELINGS IT BROUGHT UP

○ Anger   ○ Anxiety   ○ Peace

○ Fear   ○ Happiness   ○ Love

○ Shame   ○ Freedom   ○ Confusion

○ Sadness   ○ Arousal   ○ Other: _____

WHAT RECURRING THEMES OR SYMBOLS HAVE YOU IDENTIFIED?

_____

_____

_____

_____

DATE:

THE TYPE OF DREAM

○ Nightmare ○ Fantasy ○ Symbolic ○ Lucid

ANY SLEEP AIDS USED?

○ No ○ Yes: _____

SLEEP DURATION

_____ hours

WHAT HAPPENED IN THE DREAM?

_____
_____
_____
_____
_____
_____

WHAT'S YOUR INTERPRETATION?

_____
_____
_____
_____
_____
_____

REFLECTIVE DRAWING

A quick sketch that represents what happened or how you're feeling

WHAT FEELINGS IT BROUGHT UP

- ○ Anger
- ○ Fear
- ○ Shame
- ○ Sadness

- ○ Anxiety
- ○ Happiness
- ○ Freedom
- ○ Arousal

- ○ Peace
- ○ Love
- ○ Confusion
- ○ Other: _____

WHAT RECURRING THEMES OR SYMBOLS HAVE YOU IDENTIFIED?

_____

_____

_____

_____

_____

DATE:

THE TYPE OF DREAM

○ Nightmare   ○ Fantasy   ○ Symbolic   ○ Lucid

ANY SLEEP AIDS USED?

○ No   ○ Yes: _____

SLEEP DURATION

_____ hours

WHAT HAPPENED IN THE DREAM?

_____
_____
_____
_____
_____
_____

WHAT'S YOUR INTERPRETATION?

_____
_____
_____
_____
_____
_____

REFLECTIVE DRAWING

A quick sketch that represents what happened or how you're feeling

WHAT FEELINGS IT BROUGHT UP

- ○ Anger
- ○ Fear
- ○ Shame
- ○ Sadness

- ○ Anxiety
- ○ Happiness
- ○ Freedom
- ○ Arousal

- ○ Peace
- ○ Love
- ○ Confusion
- ○ Other: _____

WHAT RECURRING THEMES OR SYMBOLS HAVE YOU IDENTIFIED?

DATE:

THE TYPE OF DREAM

○ Nightmare   ○ Fantasy   ○ Symbolic   ○ Lucid

ANY SLEEP AIDS USED?

○ No   ○ Yes: _____

SLEEP DURATION

_____ hours

WHAT HAPPENED IN THE DREAM?

_____

_____

_____

_____

_____

_____

_____

WHAT'S YOUR INTERPRETATION?

_____

_____

_____

_____

_____

_____

_____

REFLECTIVE DRAWING

A quick sketch that represents what happened or how you're feeling

WHAT FEELINGS IT BROUGHT UP

○ Anger   ○ Anxiety   ○ Peace

○ Fear   ○ Happiness   ○ Love

○ Shame   ○ Freedom   ○ Confusion

○ Sadness   ○ Arousal   ○ Other: _____

WHAT RECURRING THEMES OR SYMBOLS HAVE YOU IDENTIFIED?

_____

_____

_____

_____

DATE:

THE TYPE OF DREAM

○ Nightmare ○ Fantasy ○ Symbolic ○ Lucid

ANY SLEEP AIDS USED?

○ No ○ Yes: _____

SLEEP DURATION

_____ hours

WHAT HAPPENED IN THE DREAM?

_____
_____
_____
_____
_____
_____
_____

WHAT'S YOUR INTERPRETATION?

_____
_____
_____
_____
_____
_____
_____

REFLECTIVE DRAWING

A quick sketch that represents what happened or how you're feeling

WHAT FEELINGS IT BROUGHT UP

- ○ Anger
- ○ Fear
- ○ Shame
- ○ Sadness

- ○ Anxiety
- ○ Happiness
- ○ Freedom
- ○ Arousal

- ○ Peace
- ○ Love
- ○ Confusion
- ○ Other: _____

WHAT RECURRING THEMES OR SYMBOLS HAVE YOU IDENTIFIED?

DATE:

THE TYPE OF DREAM

◯ Nightmare ◯ Fantasy ◯ Symbolic ◯ Lucid

ANY SLEEP AIDS USED?

◯ No ◯ Yes: _____

SLEEP DURATION

_____ hours

WHAT HAPPENED IN THE DREAM?

_____
_____
_____
_____
_____

WHAT'S YOUR INTERPRETATION?

_____
_____
_____
_____
_____
_____

REFLECTIVE DRAWING

A quick sketch that represents what happened or how you're feeling

WHAT FEELINGS IT BROUGHT UP

○ Anger   ○ Anxiety   ○ Peace

○ Fear   ○ Happiness   ○ Love

○ Shame   ○ Freedom   ○ Confusion

○ Sadness   ○ Arousal   ○ Other: _____

WHAT RECURRING THEMES OR SYMBOLS HAVE YOU IDENTIFIED?

DATE:

THE TYPE OF DREAM

○ Nightmare ○ Fantasy ○ Symbolic ○ Lucid

ANY SLEEP AIDS USED?

○ No ○ Yes: _____

SLEEP DURATION

_____ hours

WHAT HAPPENED IN THE DREAM?

_____
_____
_____
_____
_____
_____

WHAT'S YOUR INTERPRETATION?

_____
_____
_____
_____
_____
_____

REFLECTIVE DRAWING

A quick sketch that represents what happened or how you're feeling

WHAT FEELINGS IT BROUGHT UP

- ○ Anger
- ○ Fear
- ○ Shame
- ○ Sadness

- ○ Anxiety
- ○ Happiness
- ○ Freedom
- ○ Arousal

- ○ Peace
- ○ Love
- ○ Confusion
- ○ Other: _____

WHAT RECURRING THEMES OR SYMBOLS HAVE YOU IDENTIFIED?

_____

_____

_____

_____

DATE:

THE TYPE OF DREAM

○ Nightmare ○ Fantasy ○ Symbolic ○ Lucid

ANY SLEEP AIDS USED?

○ No ○ Yes: _____

SLEEP DURATION

_____ hours

WHAT HAPPENED IN THE DREAM?

_____

_____

_____

_____

_____

_____

WHAT'S YOUR INTERPRETATION?

_____

_____

_____

_____

_____

REFLECTIVE DRAWING

A quick sketch that represents what happened or how you're feeling

WHAT FEELINGS IT BROUGHT UP

○ Anger   ○ Anxiety   ○ Peace

○ Fear   ○ Happiness   ○ Love

○ Shame   ○ Freedom   ○ Confusion

○ Sadness   ○ Arousal   ○ Other: _____

WHAT RECURRING THEMES OR SYMBOLS HAVE YOU IDENTIFIED?

DATE:

THE TYPE OF DREAM

○ Nightmare ○ Fantasy ○ Symbolic ○ Lucid

ANY SLEEP AIDS USED?

○ No   ○ Yes: _____

SLEEP DURATION

_____ hours

WHAT HAPPENED IN THE DREAM?

_____
_____
_____
_____
_____
_____

WHAT'S YOUR INTERPRETATION?

_____
_____
_____
_____
_____
_____

REFLECTIVE DRAWING

A quick sketch that represents what happened or how you're feeling

WHAT FEELINGS IT BROUGHT UP

○ Anger   ○ Anxiety   ○ Peace

○ Fear   ○ Happiness   ○ Love

○ Shame   ○ Freedom   ○ Confusion

○ Sadness   ○ Arousal   ○ Other: _____

WHAT RECURRING THEMES OR SYMBOLS HAVE YOU IDENTIFIED?

_____

_____

_____

_____

DATE:

THE TYPE OF DREAM

◯ Nightmare ◯ Fantasy ◯ Symbolic ◯ Lucid

ANY SLEEP AIDS USED?

◯ No ◯ Yes: _____

SLEEP DURATION

_____ hours

WHAT HAPPENED IN THE DREAM?

_____
_____
_____
_____
_____
_____
_____

WHAT'S YOUR INTERPRETATION?

_____
_____
_____
_____
_____
_____

REFLECTIVE DRAWING

A quick sketch that represents what happened or how you're feeling

WHAT FEELINGS IT BROUGHT UP

○ Anger   ○ Anxiety   ○ Peace

○ Fear   ○ Happiness   ○ Love

○ Shame   ○ Freedom   ○ Confusion

○ Sadness   ○ Arousal   ○ Other: _____

WHAT RECURRING THEMES OR SYMBOLS HAVE YOU IDENTIFIED?

_____

_____

_____

_____

DATE:

THE TYPE OF DREAM

○ Nightmare ○ Fantasy ○ Symbolic ○ Lucid

ANY SLEEP AIDS USED?

○ No ○ Yes: _____

SLEEP DURATION

_____ hours

WHAT HAPPENED IN THE DREAM?

_____
_____
_____
_____
_____
_____
_____

WHAT'S YOUR INTERPRETATION?

_____
_____
_____
_____
_____
_____
_____

REFLECTIVE DRAWING

A quick sketch that represents what happened or how you're feeling

WHAT FEELINGS IT BROUGHT UP

○ Anger   ○ Anxiety   ○ Peace

○ Fear   ○ Happiness   ○ Love

○ Shame   ○ Freedom   ○ Confusion

○ Sadness ○ Arousal   ○ Other: _____

WHAT RECURRING THEMES OR SYMBOLS HAVE YOU IDENTIFIED?

_____

_____

_____

_____

_____

Made in the USA
Monee, IL
13 August 2023

40961508R00057